Duden Schülerhilfen

Englisch 4. Klasse

Texte und Übungen für die Grundstufe 2

W0385974

Bibliografische Information der Deutschen Bibliothek
Die Deutsche Bibliothek verzeichnet diese Publikation
in der Deutschen Nationalbibliografie;
detaillierte bibliografische Daten sind im Internet
über http://dnb.ddb.de abrufbar.

Das Werk wurde in neuer Rechtschreibung verfasst.

Redaktionelle Leitung: Katja Schüler
Lektorat: Birgit Hock, Ludwigshafen
Herstellerische Leitung: Claudia Rönsch
Layout: Sigrid Hecker, Mannheim
Umschlagkonzept: Bender & Büwendt, Berlin
Satz und Herstellung: Katrin Kleinschrot, Stuttgart
Druck und Bindung: Appl, Wemding
Printed in Germany
ISBN 3-411-06037-9

Duden Schülerhilfen

Englisch 4. Klasse

Texte und Übungen für die Grundstufe 2

von Kattrin Stier

mit Illustrationen von Judith Arndt

Dudenverlag

Mannheim · Leipzig · Wien · Zürich

Inhaltsverzeichnis

Einleitung

English is great

Englisch ist toll. Wie viel Spaß es macht, Englisch zu lernen, hast du inzwischen schon gemerkt. Mit diesem Buch kannst du das, was ihr im Unterricht lernt, noch weiter üben. Außerdem kannst du deine Sprachkenntnisse durch zusätzliche Wörter und Redewendungen erweitern. In diesem Buch werden geringe Vorkenntnisse in Englisch vorausgesetzt, die du entweder in der Schule oder durch die Arbeit mit dem ersten Band erworben hast.

Das Buch besteht aus 10 Kapiteln.
Auf der ersten Seite werden jeweils die neuen Wörter mithilfe von Bildern erklärt. Dann folgen vier Seiten mit Übungen, Rätseln, Spielen und Versen zum Thema. Auf der letzten Seite des Kapitels findest du ein Verzeichnis der neuen Wörter mit Aussprachehilfe und deutscher Übersetzung. Dort kannst du nachschauen, wenn du ein Wort nicht verstehst.

Zum Nachschlagen befinden sich am Schluss des Buches alphabetische Wörterverzeichnisse Englisch-Deutsch und Deutsch-Englisch, in denen du die Bedeutung von Wörtern nachlesen kannst.

Einleitung

Du kannst die Aufgaben immer gleich im Buch bearbeiten. Hierfür benutzt du am besten einen weichen Bleistift, dann kannst du Fehler ganz leicht korrigieren.

Ab Seite 72 findest du die Lösungshilfen zu den Aufgaben. Hier kannst du selbst überprüfen, ob du alles richtig gemacht hast. Natürlich erst, wenn du die Aufgabe selbst vollständig bearbeitet hast.

Das Ausrufezeichen steht bei besonders kniffligen Aufgaben.

Original englische Lieder oder Gedichte stehen in diesen Anführungszeichen. Lies dir die Texte durch und versuche sie zu verstehen. Es macht gar nichts, wenn du einzelne Wörter oder Abschnitte nicht ganz genau übersetzen kannst. Vielleicht können dir ja auch deine Eltern, Geschwister oder Lehrer den Text einmal vorlesen. Dann hörst du, wie er klingt, und kannst selbst versuchen ihn nachzusprechen.

Die Aussprache

Auf den Wortschatzseiten in diesem Buch findest du immer eine Aussprachehilfe zu den einzelnen Wörtern, die mit ganz eigenen Schriftzeichen dargestellt wird. Diese Lautschrift ist wie eine Geheimschrift, die dir genau verrät, wie das jeweilige Wort auszusprechen ist.

Am besten kann man die Aussprache natürlich lernen, indem man anderen zuhört, die die Sprache gut können. Achte genau darauf, wie deine Lehrerin oder dein Lehrer in der Schule die Wörter ausspricht, oder frage deine Eltern nach der richtigen Aussprache. Die Lautschrift im Buch ist dann eine gute Erinnerung.

Die Lautschrift

Du wirst sehen, dass die meisten Mitlaute (Konsonanten) und auch einige Selbstlaute (Vokale) im Deutschen und Englischen gleich ausgesprochen werden.

Es gibt im Englischen aber auch einige Laute, die im Deutschen nicht vorkommen. Diese werden hier vorgestellt und erklärt.

Sehr wichtig ist das th, das in der Aussprachehilfe mit den Zeichen θ oder ð geschrieben wird. Du sprichst diesen Laut wie ein s, bei dem du mit der Zunge an die Zähne stößt, so als würdest du lispeln. Du kannst den Laut üben, indem du zuerst ein t sprichst und mit der Zunge vorne am Gaumen anstößt, dann lässt du die Zunge immer weiter nach unten rutschen. Wenn sie bei deinen Zähnen angekommen ist, ist aus dem t ein echt englisches th geworden. Dabei wird das θ stimmlos, also hart und mit Nachdruck, und das ð stimmhaft, also weich, gesprochen.

Das r wird im Englischen nicht so hart gesprochen wie im Deutschen. Man formt den Mund zu einem u und kaut dann ein bisschen auf dem r herum, so als hätte man einen Kaugummi oder eine heiße Kartoffel im Mund.

Das w heißt auf Englisch double u, also doppeltes u, und so ähnlich wird es auch ausgesprochen, bei water – 'wɔːtə(r) – Wasser zum Beispiel.

Folgende Vokale haben keine genaue Entsprechung im Deutschen:

aː ist ein langes, offenes a.

ʌ ist ein kurzes a.

æ wird ähnlich ausgesprochen wie ein ä.

ɛ wird ähnlich ausgesprochen wie ein ö.

ɔː ist ein offenes o, das du vielleicht aus dem Wort Talkshow kennst.

ɒ ist ein ganz kurzes o.

Außerdem gibt es im Englischen viele Zwielaute (Diphthonge):

aɪ wie in buy – wird ähnlich ausgesprochen wie das deutsche ai.

aʊ wie in house – wird ähnlich ausgesprochen wie das deutsche au.

eɪ wie in make – wird ausgesprochen wie e-i.

ɛə wie in bear – wird ausgesprochen wie ein ä-a.

ɪə wie in ear – wird ausgesprochen wie i-ä.

ɔɪ wie in boy – wird ausgesprochen wie o-i.

Gleiches Wort – andere Aussprache

Wenn du in diesem Buch oder im Unterricht noch mehr solche ähnlichen Wörter entdeckst, kannst du sie hier eintragen.

Englisch	Deutsch
arm ɑːm	Arm
bus bʌs	Bus
butter ˈbʌtə(r)	Butter
finger ˈfiŋgə(r)	Finger
tiger ˈtaɪgə(r)	Tiger
orange ˈɒrɪndʒ	Orange

English is cool

Englisch ist cool, deswegen werden zum Beispiel in der Werbung sehr viele englische Wörter verwendet. Cool ist schon eines davon. Es heißt eigentlich kühl.

Wenn du dich beim Einkaufen einmal umschaust oder in einer Zeitschrift blätterst, kannst du bestimmt viele englische Wörter entdecken und die Liste unten ergänzen. Kennst du auch die deutsche Bedeutung der Wörter?

T-Shirt	
Cornflakes	
Computer	
Sweatshirt	
Walkman	
CD-Player	

On the telephone

Hello!

Hello, this is Lilly.
Who's there?

It's me, Ben.
Hi, Lilly, how
are you?

I'm fine, thanks,
and you?

I'm fine, too, thank you.

It's my birthday
tomorrow.

Oh, yes.

I'm having a party.

That's great.

Are you coming?

Yes, of course.

Cool, see you
tomorrow.

What time?

At five o'clock.

O.K. See you.

Bye.

1. What are they saying? Fill in the right words.

Hello!

Hi, …………………………….

……………………………….?

It's me, Anne.

H……………………………?

I'm ………………………….

……………………………….

Tomorrow is my

……………………………….

Oh, right.

I'm ………………………….

Super.

Are you …………………….?

Yes.

Great, see you

……………………………….

What ……………………….?

At …………………………….

……………………………….

……………………………….

2. Write the numbers in the book.

I'm Lilly. My telephone number is eight nine four three six seven.

I'm Ben. My telephone number is nine one nine one four three eight.

I'm Tom. My telephone number is three eight one six nine.

I'm Mary. My telephone number is seven three six five four.

What's your telephone number? I'm ....

My number is ....

3. Connect the numbers with the telephones.

eɪt faɪv sɪks 'sevn θriː eɪt

θriː 'sevn eɪt wʌn sɪks faɪv

sɪks wʌn tuː θriː eɪt wʌn

tuː faɪv faɪv naɪn 'sevn tuː

faɪv fɔː(r) tuː θriː fɔː(r) eɪt

'sevn tuː fɔː(r) θriː wʌn fɔː(r)

4. Read the poem.

Eletelephony

Once there was an elephant
Who tried to use the telephant –
No! No! I mean an elephone
Who tried to use the telephone –
(Dear me! I am not certain quite
That even now I've got it right.)
Howe'er it was, he got his trunk
Entangled in the telephunk;
The more he tried to get it free,
The louder buzzed the telephee –
(I fear I'd better drop the song
Of elephop and telephong!

Laura
Elizabeth
Richards
(1850–1943)

Vocabulary

on the telephone	ɒn ðə 'telɪfəʊn	am Telefon
This is …	ðɪs ɪz	Hier ist …
Who's there?	huːz ðeə(r)	Wer ist dort?
It's me.	ɪts mɪ	Ich bin's.
thanks	θæŋks	danke
too	tuː	auch
tomorrow	tə'mɒrəʊ	morgen
I'm having a party.	aɪm hævɪŋ ə pɑːtɪ	Ich mache eine Party.
great	greɪt	toll
Are you coming?	ɑː(r) jʊ 'kʌmɪŋ	Kommst du?
of course	əv kɔːs	natürlich
What time?	wɒt taɪm	um wie viel Uhr?
at 5 o'clock	ət faɪv ə'klɒk	um 5 Uhr
right	raɪt	stimmt
What's your number?	jə(r) 'nʌmbə(r)	Wie ist deine Nummer?
telephone number	'telɪfəʊn 'nʌmbə(r)	die Telefonnummer
Read the poem!	riːd ðə 'pəʊɪm	Lies das Gedicht!
Once there was …	wʌns ðeə(r) wəz	Es war einmal ...
… who tried	hʊ traɪd	… der versuchte
to use something	tʊ juːs səmθɪŋ	etwas benutzen
I mean.	aɪ miːn	Ich meine
Dear me!	dɪə(r) miː	Oh je!
not quite certain	nɒt kwaɪt 'sɜːtn	nicht ganz sicher
even now	'iːvn naʊ	selbst jetzt
I've got it right.	aɪv gɒt ɪt raɪt	Jetzt hab ich es richtig.
howe'er/however	haʊ'evə(r)	wie auch immer
It was …	ɪt wɒz	Es war …
his trunk	hɪs trʌŋk	sein Rüssel
entangled	ɪn'tæŋgld	verknotet, verwickelt
the more … the louder	ðə mɔː(r) ... ðə laʊdə(r)	je mehr … desto lauter
buzzed	bʌzd	läutete
I fear	aɪ fɪər	Ich fürchte
I'd better drop the song.	aɪd 'betə(r) drɒp ðə sɒŋ	Ich lasse das Lied lieber weg.

Opposites

cold
hot
old
new
clean
dirty
dry
wet
sad
happy
light
long
short
black
white
heavy
big
small
young
old
right
left

1. Fill in.

The snowman is cold

and white.

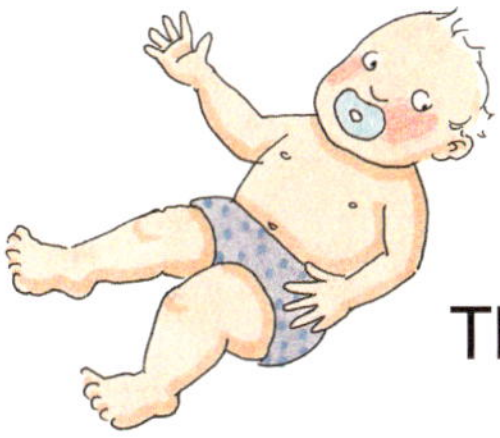

The baby is _____.

The ladybird is _____.

The girl is ___.

The boy is _____.

The bird is _____.

The bear is ___.

The witch is ___.

2. Connect the opposites.

cold	sad
new	old
white	light
long	black
heavy	dry
small	right
happy	short
old	hot
clean	big
wet	young
left	dirty

3. Crossword puzzle

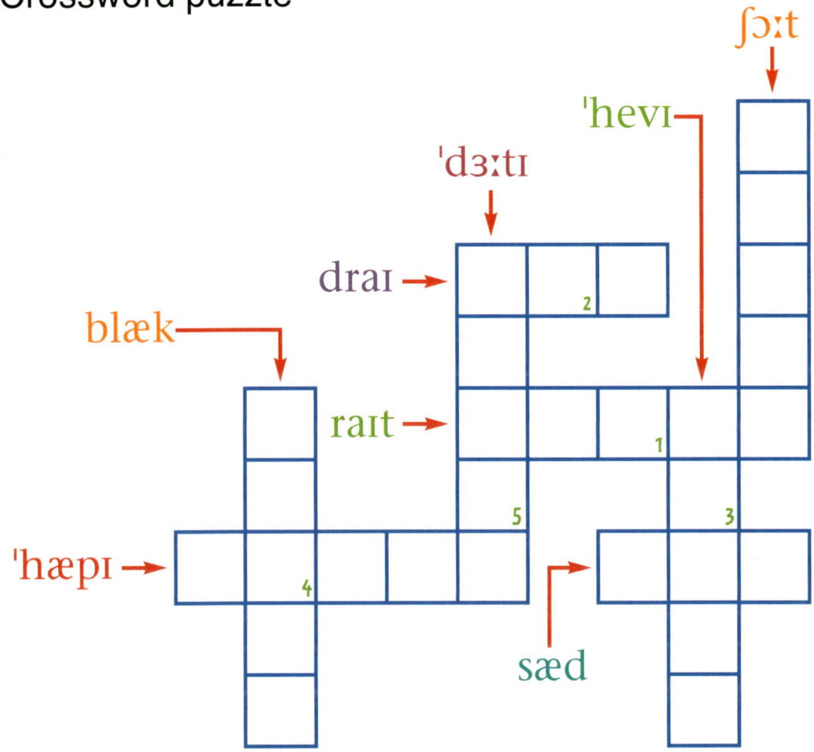

4. Read the text. Do you know the song?

If you're happy and you know it

If you're happy and you know it
Clap your hands. (clap clap)
If you're happy and you know it
Clap your hands. (clap clap)
If you're happy and you know it
Then you really ought to show it.
If you're happy and you know it
Clap your hands. (clap clap)

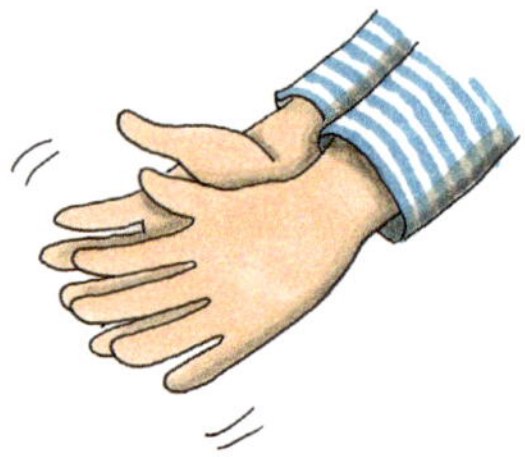

If you're happy and you know it
Stamp your feet. (stamp stamp)
If you're happy and you know it
Stamp your feet. (stamp stamp)
If you're happy and you know it
Then you really ought to show it.
If you're happy and you know it
Stamp your feet. (stamp stamp)

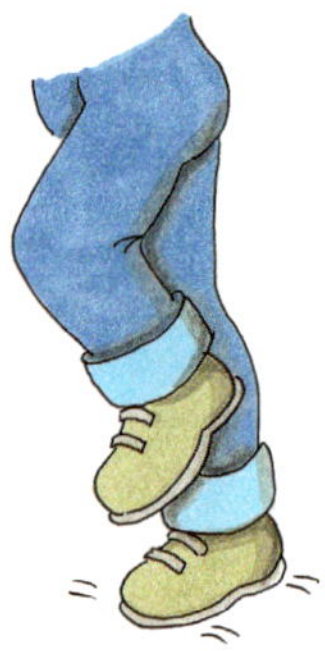

If you're happy and you know it
Shout hurray: Hurray!
If you're happy and you know it
Shout hurray: Hurray!
If you're happy and you know it
Then you really ought to show it.
If you're happy and you know it
Shout hurray: Hurray!

Vocabulary

opposites 'ɒpəzɪtz	die Gegensätze
old əʊld	alt
young jʌŋ	jung
new njuː	neu
long lɒŋ	lang
short ʃɔːt	kurz
clean kliːn	sauber
dirty 'dɜːtɪ	dreckig
happy 'hæpɪ	glücklich
sad sæd	traurig
hot hɒt	heiß
cold kəʊld	kalt
heavy 'hevɪ	schwer
light laɪt	leicht
wet wet	nass
dry draɪ	trocken
snowman snəʊmæn	der Schneemann
witch wɪtʃ	die Hexe
Do you know the song? duː jʊ nəʊ ðə sɒŋ	Kennst du das Lied?
If you're happpy and you know it, ɪf jə(r) 'hæpɪ and jʊ nəʊ ɪt	Wenn du glücklich bist und du weißt es,
then you really ought to show it. ðen jʊ 'rɪəlɪ ɔːt tə ʃəʊ ɪt	dann solltest du es wirklich zeigen.
Clap your hands! klæp jə(r) hændz	Klatsche in die Hände!
Stamp your feet! stæmp jə(r) fiːt	Stampfe mit den Füßen!
Shout hurray! ʃaʊt hə'reɪ	Rufe hurra!

Clothes

underwear
sweatshirt
T-shirt
jeans
trousers
jumper
dress
coat
jacket
socks
shoes
belt
scarf
hat
skirt
gloves
cap
boots
sandals

1. What are you wearing today?

Doodoo is wearing a
b l u e T - s h i r t.

Bob is wearing a _ _ _ _ sweatshirt and
green _ _ _ _ _ _ _ _.
His shoes are _ _ _ _ _.

Lilly is wearing a white _ _ _ _ _ _ _
and a _ _ _ skirt. Her shoes are _ _ _ _.

Ben is wearing a _ _ _ _ _ _
_ _ _ _ _ _ _ and _ _ _ _
_ _ _ _ _ _ _ _.
His shoes are _ _ _ _ _.

Anne is wearing a _ _ _ _ _ _ _ _ _.
Her shoes are _ _ _ _ _.

What are you wearing today? I am wearing ....
.... My shoes are ....

2. What's in Doodoos washing machine?

Doodoo lost his pink socks. Can you find them in this chapter?

There's a blue skirt.

There are ____ __________.

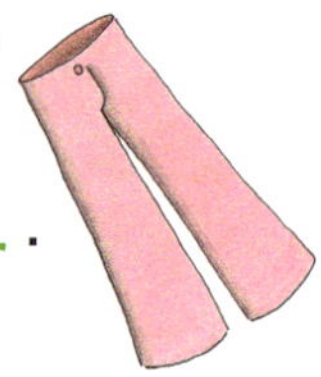

There's a ______ __________.

There's a ________ ______.

There's a ____ ____.

There's a ______ __________.

There are ______ ______.

3. What’s on Doodoos washing line?

4. Read the poem.

Diddle, diddle dumpling, my son John
went to bed with his trousers on,
one sock off and one sock on,
diddle, diddle dumpling, my son John.

5. Colour the picture.

Colour the curtain blue and yellow.

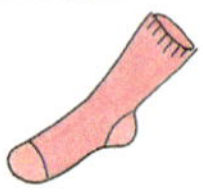

Colour the trousers brown.

Colour the boots green.

Colour the socks blue and yellow.

Colour the jacket red.

Colour the T-shirt green.

Colour the skarf red and orange.

Colour the hat black.

Colour the dress orange and pink.

Vocabulary

clothes	kləʊðz	die Kleider
jeans	dʒiːnz	die Jeans
T-shirt	'tiːʃəːt	das T-Shirt
sweatshirt	'swɛtʃəːt	das Sweatshirt
jumper	'dʒʌmpə(r)	der Pulli
coat	kəʊt	der Mantel
dress	dres	das Kleid
skirt	skɜːt	der Rock
trousers	'traʊzəz	die Hose
gloves	glʌvz	die Handschuhe
scarf	skɑːf	der Schal
hat	hæt	der Hut/die Mütze
cap	kæp	die Kappe
underwear	'ʌndə(r)weə(r)	die Unterwäsche
belt	belt	der Gürtel
shoes	ʃuːz	die Schuhe
boots	buːts	Stiefel
sandals	'sændlz	die Sandalen
socks	sɒks	die Socken
What are you wearing?	wɒt ɑː(r) jʊ 'weərɪŋ	Was trägst du?
… is wearing …	ɪz 'weərɪŋ	… trägt …
I am wearing …	aɪ əm 'weərɪŋ	Ich trage …
washing machine	'wɒʃɪŋ mə'ʃiːn	die Waschmaschine
washing line	'wɒʃɪŋ laɪn	die Wäscheleine
diddle, diddle, dumpling	'dɪdl 'dɪdl 'dʌmplɪŋ	Kniddel, Knaddel, Knödel
my son	maɪ sʌn	mein Sohn
He went to bed.	hɪ went tə bed	Er ging ins Bett.
off	ɒf	aus, ab
on	ɒn	an
Doodoo lost his socks.	dudu lɒst hɪz sɒks	Doodoo hat seine Socken verloren.
Can you find them?	kæn jʊ faɪnd ðəm	Kannst du sie finden?
chapter	'tʃæptə(r)	das Kapitel

What time is it?

1. Draw the right time.

It's nine o'clock.

It's a quarter past five.

It's ten o'clock.

It's half past eleven.

It's a quarter to two.

It's half past three.

It's four o'clock.

It's a quarter to six.

It's a quarter past seven.

2. Hickory, dickory, dock.
Read the poem and answer the questions.

Hickory, dickory, dock!
The mouse ran up the clock.
The clock struck one,
the mouse ran down.
Hickory, dickory, dock!

Hickory, dickory, dock!
The mouse ran up the clock.
The clock struck two,
the mouse said "boo".
Hickory, dickory, dock.

Hickory, dickory, dock!
The mouse ran up the clock.
The clock struck four,
the mouse said "no more".
Hickory, dickory, dock.

The mouse said "no more"

- ☐ at four o'clock.
- ☐ at three o'clock.
- ☐ at five o'clock.

The mouse ran down

- ☐ at two o'clock.
- ☐ at one o'clock.
- ☐ at six o'clock.

3. What's the time, please?

What are they saying? Fill in the right words.

Excuse me, what's the time, please? It's a quarter past

....

Excuse me, what's the time, please? It's ....

....

Excuse me, ...

................? ....

....

....

................? ....

....

4. Connect the picture and the time.

a quarter past four

half past eleven

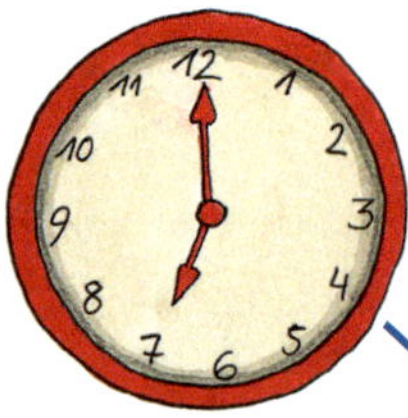

a quarter to ten

six o'clock

two o'clock

seven o'clock

a quarter to two

half past three

Vocabulary

What time is it? wɒt taɪm ɪz ɪt	Wie viel Uhr ist es?
clock klɒk	die Uhr
watch wɒtʃ	die Armbanduhr
It's … o'clock ɪts ... əˈklɒk	Es ist … Uhr.
a quarter to … ə ˈkwɔːtə(r) tə	Viertel vor
a quarter past ə ˈkwɔːtə(r) pɑːst	Viertel nach
half past hɑːf pɑːst	halb
Answer the questions. ˈɑːnsə(r) ðə ˈkwestʃnz	Beantworte die Fragen.
the mouse ran up ðə maʊs ræn ʌp	die Maus rannte hinauf
the mouse ran down ðə maʊs ræn daʊn	die Maus rannte hinunter
the clock struck ðə klɒk strʌk	die Uhr schlug
no more nəʊ mɔː(r)	genug
Excuse me! ɪkˈskjuːz mɪ	Entschuldige/ Entschuldigen Sie!
What's the time, please? wɒts ðə taɪm pliːz	Wie spät ist es, bitte?

t school

MONDAY TUESDAY WEDNESDAY THURSDAY FRIDAY SATURDAY
1. 2. 3. 4. 5. 6. 7. 8. 9. 10.
timetable
classroom
book
exercise book
schoolbag
pen
ruler
pencil
chair
desk
rubber
chalk
pupil
teacher
blackboard

1. Connect.

d s k e

b e r b r u

l r a m s c s o o

e c l p n i

u l p p i

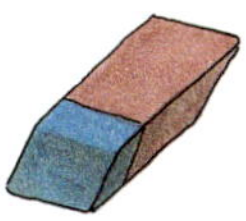

l r e r u

e h r a c e t

2. Playtime. Guess the word.

You play this game with a friend.

You think of a word in English.

You draw a line for every letter.

Your friend has to guess a letter.

For every wrong letter you draw a line.

When the house is complete – you are the winner.

When the word is complete – your friend is the winner.

Here are more words for the game:

yellow	orange	penguin	armchair
wardrobe	strawberry	bathroom	telephone
schoolbag	blackboard	timetable	alphabet

Think of your own words!

3. Find 10 words.

p	e	b	a	x	y	z	u	p	e	n	l	a	d	i
d	f	b	n	r	o	g	s	l	p	v	q	c	o	n
e	d	o	v	r	u	l	e	r	e	g	j	m	c	d
k	y	o	x	t	k	k	d	b	a	o	b	c	h	o
l	a	k	r	i	v	y	k	u	p	t	e	f	a	q
s	u	z	s	c	h	o	o	l	b	a	g	v	l	u
m	d	e	z	u	s	m	p	r	l	d	h	i	k	p
a	d	f	h	j	o	s	y	l	a	n	t	e	b	y
p	e	p	u	r	h	q	u	i	c	n	o	c	a	f
u	b	y	d	e	s	k	s	a	k	r	n	h	b	e
p	j	o	h	s	b	e	r	y	b	l	n	a	x	i
i	x	c	r	y	s	a	g	z	o	k	v	i	c	b
l	a	z	t	s	u	w	u	l	a	m	t	r	h	o
o	t	e	a	c	h	e	r	i	r	d	e	l	i	o
t	a	e	g	c	u	l	m	o	d	r	a	g	l	l

Vocabulary

at school ət skuːl	in der Schule
classroom klɑːsrʊm	das Klassenzimmer
teacher ˈtiːtʃə(r)	der Lehrer/die Lehrerin
pupil ˈpjuːpɪl	der Schüler/die Schülerin
schoolbag skuːlbæg	die Schultasche
chair tʃeə(r)	der Stuhl
desk desk	der Schreibtisch/das Pult
pen pen	der Stift
pencil ˈpensɪl	der Bleistift
ruler ˈruːlə(r)	das Lineal
rubber ˈrʌbə(r)	der Radiergummi
exercise book ˈeksəsaɪz bʊk	das Schreibheft
book bʊk	das Buch
blackboard blækbɔːd	die Tafel
chalk tʃɔːk	die Kreide
timetable taɪmˈteɪbl	der Stundenplan
alphabet ˈælfəbet	das Alphabet
letters letə(r)z	die Buchstaben
playtime pleɪtaɪm	die Spielzeit
Guess the word! ges ðə wɜːd	Errate das Wort!
you play jʊ pleɪ	du spielst
game geɪm	das Spiel
with wɪð	mit
You think of a word. jʊ θɪŋk əv ə wɜːd	Du denkst dir ein Wort aus.
You draw a line for every letter. jʊ drɔː ə laɪn fə(r) ˈevrɪ letə(r)	Du machst für jeden Buchstaben einen Strich.
Your friend has to guess … jə(r) frend hæz tə ges	Dein Freund/deine Freundin muss raten …
for every wrong letter fə(r) ˈevrɪ rɒŋ letə(r)	für jeden falschen Buchstaben
when the house is wen ðə haʊs ɪz	wenn das Haus
complete kəmˈpliːt	vollständig ist
winner ˈwɪnə(r)	der Gewinner
more mɔː(r)	mehr
Think of your own words! θɪŋk əv jə(r) əʊn wɜːdz	Denke dir selbst Wörter aus!

in
behind
on
under
in front of
next to
between

1. Where are the Easter eggs?
Fill in the right words and colour the eggs.

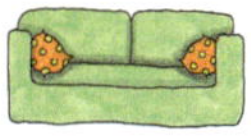 Doodoo is b e h i n d the sofa.

There is a green egg __ __ the table. 

There is a pink egg __ __ the bowl. 

There is a grey egg
__ __ __ __ __ __ the armchair. 

There is a red egg __ __
__ __ __ __ __ __ __ the lamp. 

There is a blue egg __ __ __ __ __ the rug. 

There is an orange egg
__ __ __ __ __ __ __ the books. 

2. Easter Sunday

Where is Doodoo?

Can you see his tail?

I can see Doodoo's tail

in .... pictures.

3. Crossword puzzle

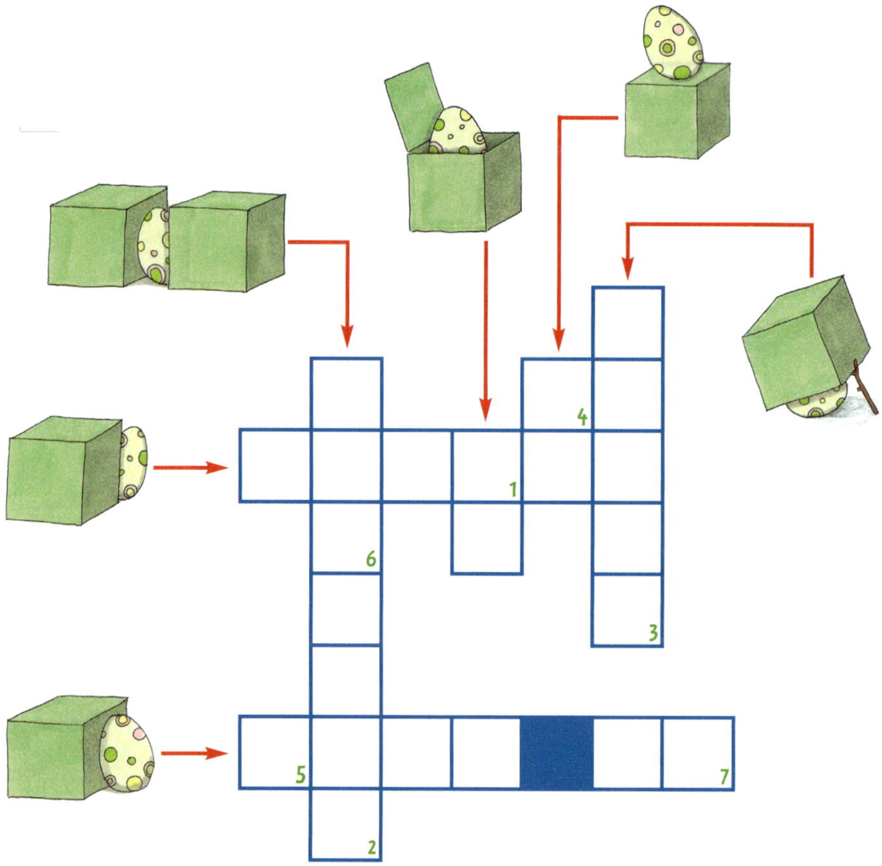

Vocabulary

Easter ˈiːstə(r)	Ostern
in ɪn	in
on ɒn	auf
under ˈʌndə(r)	unter
behind bɪˈhaɪnd	hinter
in front of ɪn frʌnt əv	vor
next to nekst tə	neben
between bɪˈtwiːn	zwischen
Where are …? weə(r) ə(r)	Wo sind …?
Easter eggs ˈiːstə(r) egz	die Ostereier
Easter Sunday ˈiːstə(r) ˈsʌndɪ	der Ostersonntag
I am late. aɪ əm leɪt	Ich bin spät dran.
I have to hurry. aɪ hæv tə ˈhʌrɪ	Ich muss mich beeilen.
I will put the eggs … aɪ wɪl pʊt ðɪ egz	Ich werde die Eier … legen.
now naʊ	jetzt
Look for your Easter eggs! lʊk fə(r) jə(r) ˈiːstə(r) egz	Sucht eure Ostereier!
I will sit down. aɪ wɪl sɪt daʊn	Ich werde mich hinsetzen.
There are no … ðeə(r) ə(r) nəʊ	Es sind keine …/ Es gibt keine …
We can't find … wɪ kaːnt faɪnd	Wir können … nicht finden.
impossible ɪmˈpɒsɪbl	unmöglich
O dear! əʊ dɪə(r)	Oh je!
Look at that! lʊk ət ðæt	Seht euch das an!
… times taɪmz	…mal

Summer holidays

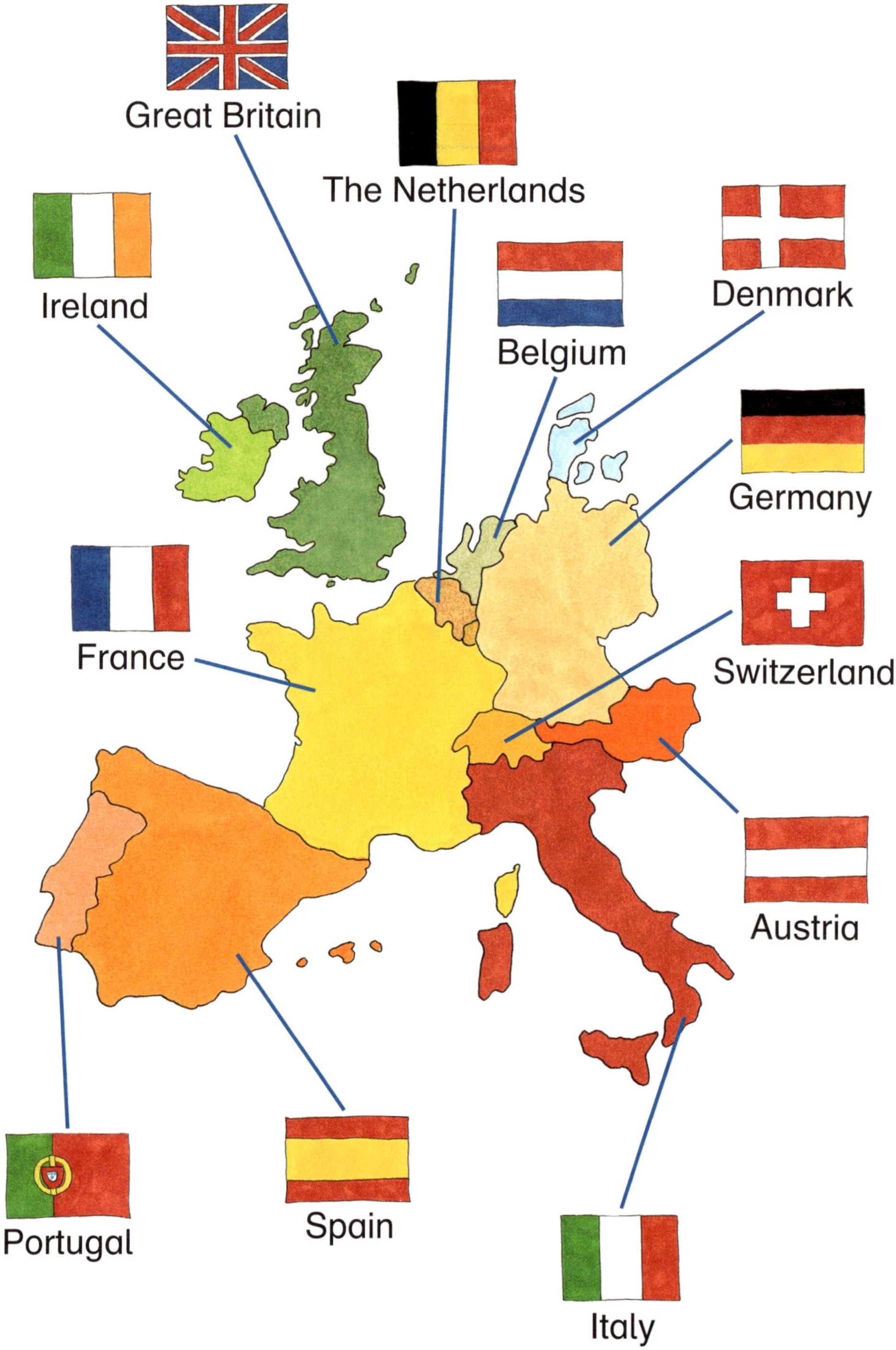

1. Where do you live? Where are you going on holiday?

I live in G r e a t B r i t a i n. 

We are going on holiday to F r a n c e. 

I live in _ _ _ _ _ _ _ _ _ _ _ _. 

We are going on holiday to _ _ _ _ _ _ _. 

I live in _ _ _ _ _. 

We are going on holiday to _ _ _ _ _ _ _. 

I live in _ _ _ _ _ _ _. 

We are going on holiday to _ _ _ _ _. 

I live in _ _ _ _ _ _. 

We are going on holiday to _ _ _ _ _ _ _. 

Where do you live? ....

We are going on holiday to ....

2. Colour the flags.

Colour the flag blue, red and white.

It's the flag of □□□□□ □□□□□□□.

Colour the flag red an yellow.

It's the flag of □□□□□.

Colour the flag green, white and red.

It's the flag of □□□□□.

Colour the flag blue, red and white.

It's the flag of □□□□□□.

Colour the flag black, red and gold (yellow).

It's the flag of □□□□□□□.

3. Transport

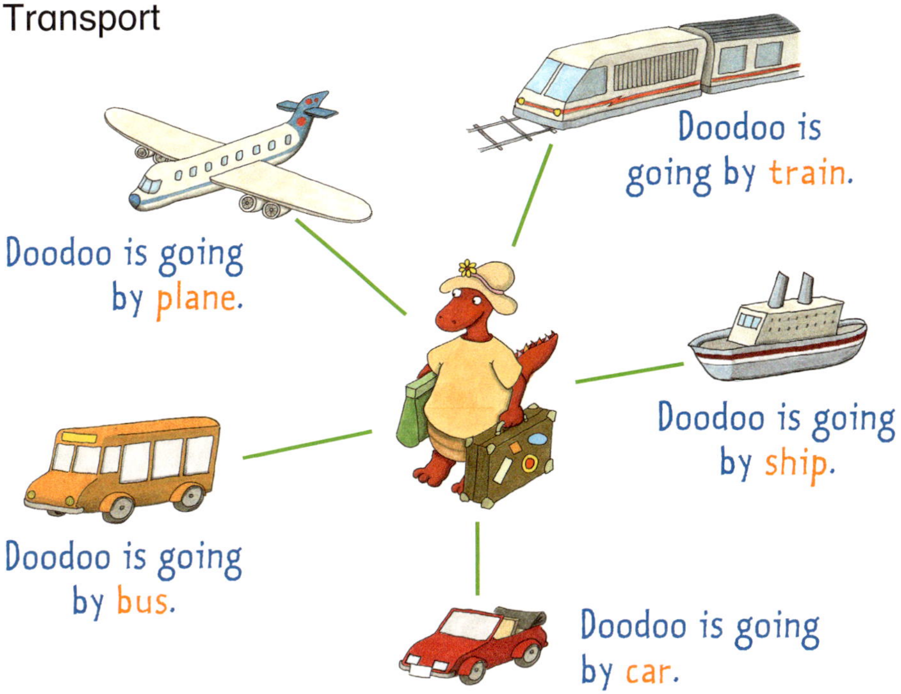

Bob is going __ ___ . 

Anne and Lilly are ______
__ ____ . 

Judy __ _____ __ ___ . 

Mary __ _____
__ _____ . 

Ben and Tom ___ _____
__ _____ . 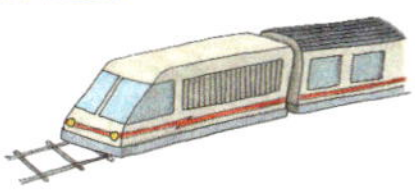

4. Crossword puzzle

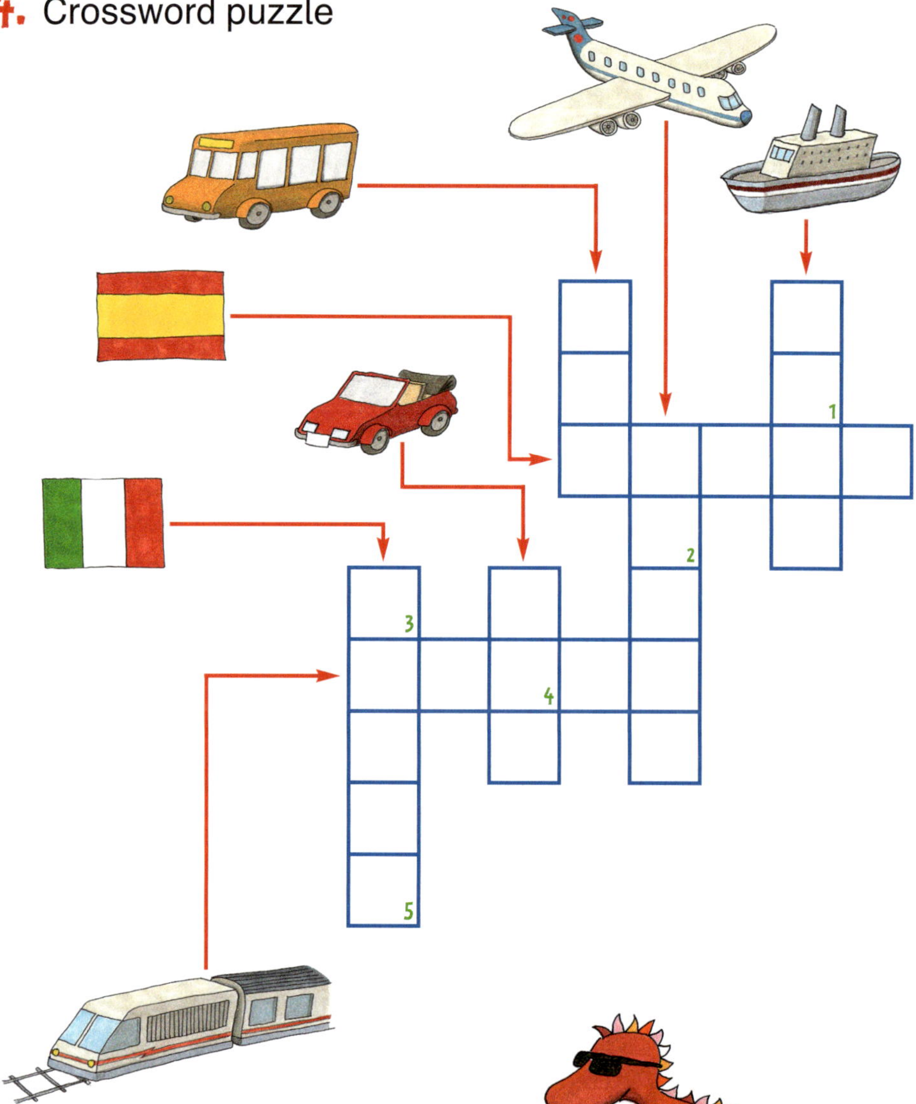

Vocabulary

summer holidays	'sʌmə(r) 'hɒlɪdeɪz	die Sommerferien
Great Britain	greɪt 'brɪtn	Großbritannien
France	frɑːns	Frankreich
Ireland	'aɪələnd	Irland
the Netherlands	ðə 'neðələndz	die Niederlande
Belgium	'beldʒəm	Belgien
Spain	speɪn	Spanien
Italy	'ɪtəlɪ	Italien
Germany	'dʒɜːmənɪ	Deutschland
Denmark	'denmɑːk	Dänemark
Austria	'ɒstrɪə	Österreich
Switzerland	'swɪtsələnd	die Schweiz
Where do you live?	weə(r) də jʊ lɪv	Wo wohnst du?
Where are you going?	weə(r) ɑː(r) jʊ 'gəʊɪŋ	Wohin fährst du?
on holiday	ɒn 'hɒlɪdeɪ	in die Ferien
We are going to …	wɪ ɑː(r) 'gəʊɪŋ tʊ	Wir gehen/fahren nach …
flag	flæg	die Flagge
transport	træn'spɔːt	das Transportmittel
Portugal	'pɔːtjʊgl	Portugal
plane	pleɪn	das Flugzeug
car	kɑː(r)	das Auto
bus	bʌs	der Bus
train	treɪn	der Zug
ship	ʃɪp	das Schiff
… is going by …	ɪz 'gəʊɪŋ baɪ	… fährt/fliegt mit dem …

Halloween

black hat
bat
spider
candle
broom
black
cat
pumpkin
ghost
cauldron
witch

1. Fill in the right word.

kæt

bruːm

ˈspaɪdə(r)

hæləʊˈiːn

bæt

wɪtʃ

2. Find the words.

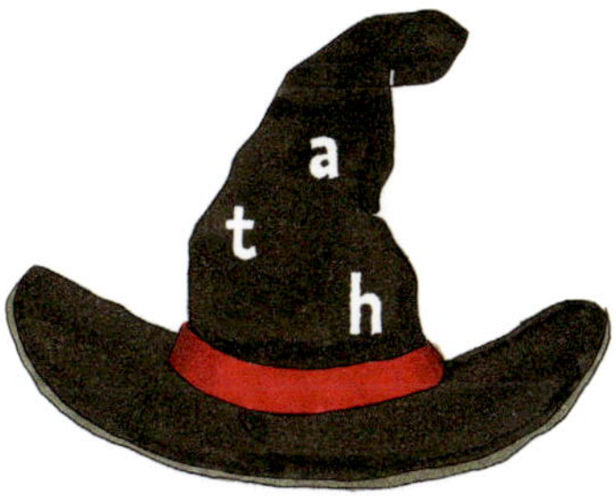

3. Halloween cakes

Ben and Lilly want to make Halloween cakes for the party. They need:

Ben puts the 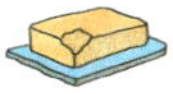 _ _ _ _ _ _ ,

the 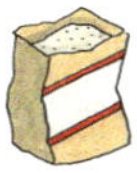 _ _ _ _ _ ,  a pinch of _ _ _ _ ,

 the _ _ _ _ ,  the _ _ _ _ _ ,

 the _ _ _ _ _ _ _ _ _ _ _ _

and the  _ _ _ _ in a bowl.

Lilly mixes everything together.

Ben puts _ _ _ _ _ _ _ _ _ _ _ on a _ _ _ _ _ _ _ _ _ _ _ .

Ben and Lilly form small balls and put them on the baking sheet.

They put the cakes in the oven and bake them for 15–20 minutes at 180 °C.

They decorate the cakes with icing.

4. When is ...?

When is Easter? 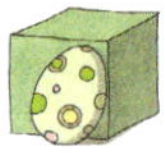

E a s t e r is in M a r c h or

A p r i l. It is in s p r i n g.

When is Halloween? 

Halloween is in _ _ _ _ _ _ _.

It is in _ _ _ _ _ _.

When is Christmas? 

Christmas is in _ _ _ _ _ _ _ _.

It is in _ _ _ _ _ _.

When is your birthday? 

It is in ....

....

When is your friend's birthday? 

It is in ....

....

Vocabulary

Halloween	hæləʊ'iːn	Halloween – die Nacht vom 31. Oktober auf den 1. November. Es ist All Hallows' Evening – die Nacht vor Allerheiligen.
witch	wɪtʃ	die Hexe
pumpkin	'pʌmpkɪn	der Kürbis
broom	bruːm	der Besen
spider	'spaɪdə(r)	die Spinne
bat	bæt	die Fledermaus
ghost	gəʊst	der Geist
cauldron	'kɔːldrən	der Kessel
cakes	keɪkz	der Kuchen
butter	'bʌtə(r)	die Butter
a pinch of salt	ə pɪnʃ əv sɒlt	eine Prise Salz
flour	flaʊə(r)	das Mehl
baking powder	'beɪkɪŋ 'paʊdə(r)	das Backpulver
tablespoon	'teɪblspuːn	der Esslöffel
some	səm	etwas
water	'wɔːtə(r)	das Wasser
icing sugar	'aɪsɪŋ 'ʃʊgə(r)	der Puderzucker
icing	'aɪsɪŋ	der Zuckerguss
mixer	'mɪksə(r)	das Handrührgerät
baking sheet	'beɪkɪŋ ʃiːt	das Backblech
baking paper	'beɪkɪŋ 'peɪpə(r)	das Backpapier
… form small balls.	fɔːm smɔːl bɔːlz	… formen kleine Bälle.
to put	tʊ pʊt	setzen, legen
They bake …	ðeɪ beɪk	Sie backen …
for … minutes	fə(r) … 'mɪnɪtz	… Minuten lang
to decorate	tʊ 'dekəreɪt	verzieren, dekorieren

The weather

clouds

It's cloudy.

rain

It's rainy.

sun

It's sunny.

snow

It's snowy.

fog

It's foggy.

wind

It's windy.

storm

It's stormy.

1. The weather forecast

Fill in the right words.

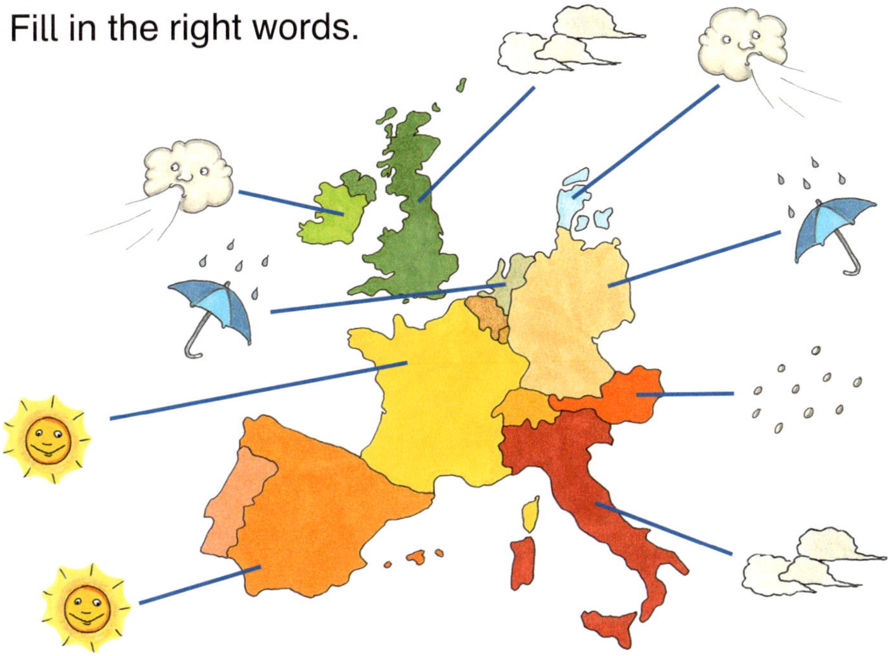

It's .... rainy .... in Germany.

It's .... in France.

It's .... in Great Britain.

It's .... in Austria.

It's .... in Denmark.

It's .... in the Netherlands.

It's .... in Italy.

It's .... in Spain.

It's .... in Ireland.

2. Connect.

It's windy.

It's rainy.

It's snowy.

It's stormy.

It's cloudy.

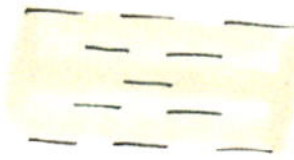

It's foggy.

It's sunny.

3. What is it?

It is cold. It is white.

It has two black _ _ _ _ _ . 

It is holding a _ _ _ _ _ . 

Its _ _ _ _  is a _ _ _ _ _ _ . 

It has no _ _ _ _ . 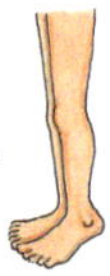

It has a black _ _ _ on the head. 

It is a N∀WMONS.

4. Ben's weather chart.

date	Monday	Tuesday	Wednesday	Thursday	Friday	Saturday	Sunday
7-4-2003 to 13-4-2003	rain	sun	clouds	fog	rain	storm	wind
14-4-2003 to 20-4-2003	sun						

Ben's weather chart

Fill in the days.

It was foggy on _ _ _ _ _ _ _ _ . It was rainy

on _ _ _ _ _ _ and on _ _ _ _ _ _ .

It was sunny on _ _ _ _ _ _ and on

_ _ _ _ _ _ _ .

It was stormy on _ _ _ _ _ _ _ _ .

What was the weather like?

On Tuesday it was _ _ _ _ _ .

On Saturday it was _ _ _ _ _ _ .

On Sunday it was _ _ _ _ _ .

On Wednesday it was _ _ _ _ _ _ .

5. Find the wrong word.

It's raining. We need

- ☐ an umbrella
- ☐ rubber boots
- ☐ a bathing suit
- ☐ a raincoat

It's snowing. We need

- ☐ winter boots
- ☐ an anorak
- ☐ a cap and gloves
- ☐ a raincoat

It's sunny. We need

- ☐ a bathing suit
- ☐ a scarf
- ☐ sunglasses
- ☐ a sunshade

It's windy. We need

- ☐ a headband
- ☐ a scarf
- ☐ sunglasses
- ☐ a jacket

Vocabulary

weather 'weðə(r)	das Wetter
rain reɪn	der Regen
rainy 'reɪnɪ	regnerisch
wind wɪnd	der Wind
windy 'wɪndɪ	windig
sun sʌn	die Sonne
sunny 'sʌnɪ	sonnig
storm stɔːm	der Sturm
stormy stɔːmɪ	stürmisch
snow snəʊ	der Schnee
snowy 'snəʊɪ	verschneit
fog fɒg	der Nebel
foggy 'fɒgɪ	neblig
clouds klaʊdz	die Wolken
cloudy 'klaʊdɪ	bewölkt
weather forecast 'weðə(r) fɔː(r)kaːst	die Wettervorhersage
It's holding a … ɪts 'həʊldɪŋ ə	Es hält ein(en) …
snowman snəʊmæn	der Schneemann
weather chart 'weðə(r) tʃaːt	die Wetterliste
days deɪz	die Tage
What was the weather like? wɒt wəz ðə 'weðə(r) laɪk	Wie war das Wetter?
umbrella ʌm'brelə	der Regenschirm
rubber boots 'rʌbə(r) buːts	die Gummistiefel
bathing suit 'beɪðɪŋ suːt	der Badeanzug
raincoat reɪnkəʊt	der Regenmantel
sunglasses sʌnglaːsɪz	die Sonnenbrille
sunshade sʌnʃeɪd	der Sonnenschirm
winter boots 'wɪntə(r) buːts	die Winterstiefel
anorak 'ænəræk	der Anorak
headband hedbænd	das Stirnband

Where to go?

left   right

turn left   turn right

straight on

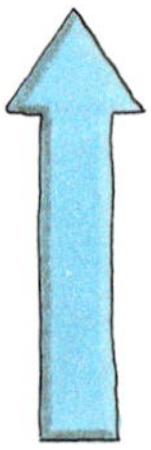

second crossing

first crossing

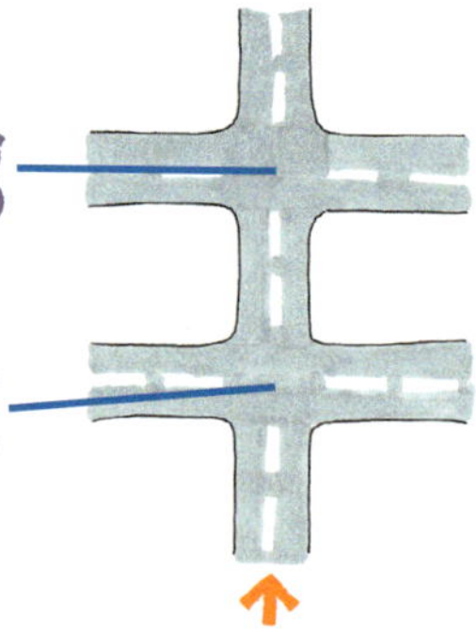

traffic lights

bus stop

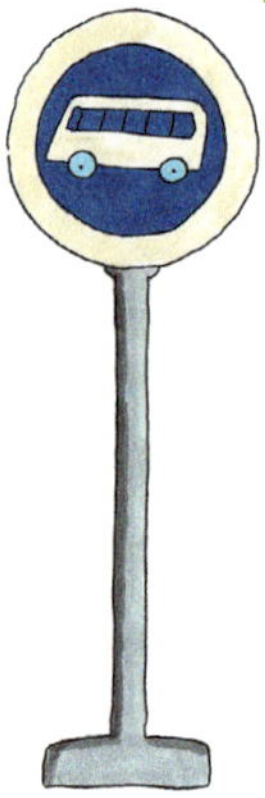

Lilly is crossing the street.

1. Find your way through the labyrinth.

You go straight on at the  . Turn right at the  .

Turn right at the  . Turn left at the second crossing. Turn left at the first crossing.

Straight on at the 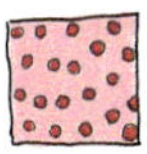 . Turn left at the 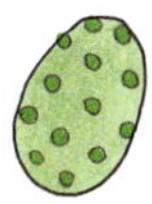 .

Straight on to the 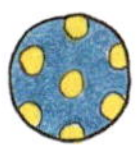 . Turn left.

Straight on at the first and at the second crossing.

There is the ☐  ☐ 

2. Lilly goes to school.

She turns right and walks to the traffic lights. There she crosses the street. She walks straight on. At the first crossing she turns left and walks to the traffic lights. She crosses the street. There is her school.

Ben goes to school. Describe his way.

He turns ______________ . At the first crossing he

turns ___________ . At the second crossing he walks

__________________________ ______ . He crosses the street

at the _ _ _ _ _ _ _ _ _ _ _ _ _ .

He walks straight on. At the first

_ _ _ _ _ _ _ _ he turns _ _ _ _ and

walks to the traffic lights. He _ _ _ _ _ _ _

_ _ _ _ _ _ _ _ _ . There is his school.

3. What are they saying? Fill in the right words.

"Excuse me, can you tell me the way from the school to the bus stop, please?" "Yes, you turn left and go straight on, at the first crossing you _ _ _ _

_ _ _ _ _. There's the bus stop." "Thank you."

"Excuse _ _, can _ _ _ tell _ _ the _ _ _ from the bus stop to the school, please?"

"Yes, you _ _ s_ _ _ _ _ _ _ on.

At the first crossing _ _ _ _ _ _ _

_ _ _ _ _ . T_ _ _ _ '_ the school."

4. Connect the picture with the right words.

straight on

turn right

right

turn left

bus stop

traffic lights

crossing

left

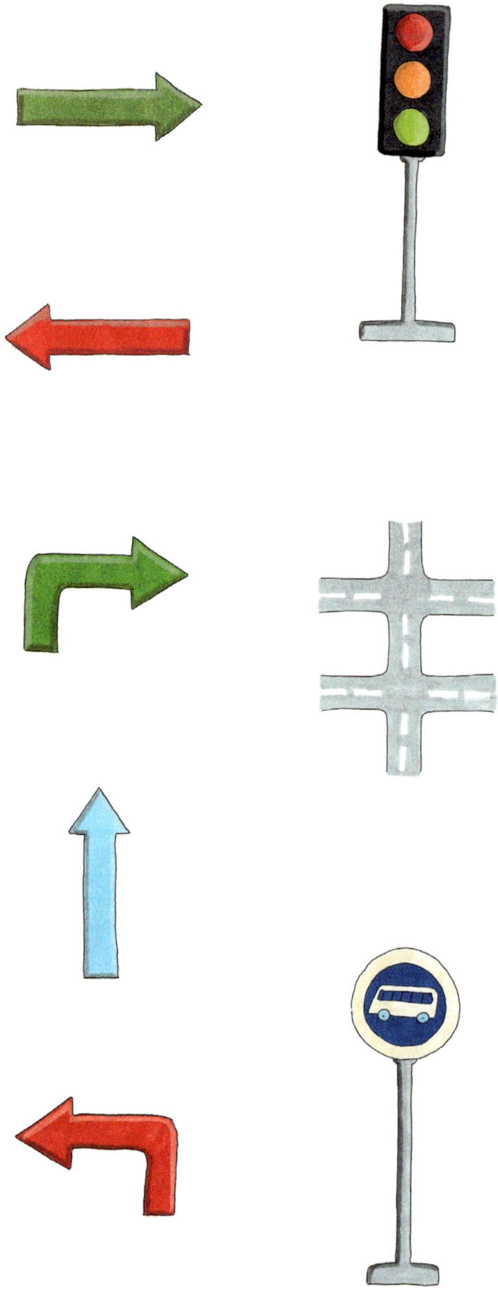

Vocabulary

Where to go? wɛə(r) tə gəʊ	Wohin?
right raɪt	rechts
left left	links
turn right/left tɜːn raɪt/left	rechts/links abbiegen
straight on streɪt ɒn	geradeaus
first/second crossing fɜːst/'sekənd 'krɒsɪŋ	die erste/zweite Kreuzung
traffic lights 'træfɪk laɪtz	Ampel
Lilly is crossing the street. lɪlɪ ɪz 'krɒsɪŋ ðə striːt	Lilly geht über die Straße.
bus stop bʌs 'stɒp	die Bushaltestelle
Find your way … faɪnd jə(r) weɪ	Finde deinen Weg …
through θruː	durch
labyrinth 'læbərɪnθ	das Labyrinth
Lilly goes to school. lɪlɪ gəʊz tə skuːl	Lilly geht zur Schule.
Describe his way! dɪ'skraɪb hɪz weɪ	Beschreibe seinen Weg!
Can you tell me …? kæn jʊ tel mɪ	Können Sie mir sagen/ Kannst du mir sagen …?
the way from the school to the bus stop ðə weɪ frəm ðə skuːl tə ðə bʌs 'stɒp	der Weg von der Schule zur Bushaltestelle

Lösungshilfen

In diesem Teil findest du für die meisten Aufgaben Lösungen oder Vorschläge, die du mit deinen eigenen Lösungen vergleichen kannst.

Seite 11

T-shirt heißt so viel wie T-Hemd, weil es ausgebreitet ungefähr die Form eines Ts hat. Cornflakes sind Maisflocken. Ein Computer ist ein Rechner. Sweatshirt heißt wörtlich übersetzt Schweißhemd. Es war ursprünglich eine reine Sportkleidung. Walkman ist ein Geh-Mann, also ein Kassettenrekorder, bei dem man auch unterwegs, beim Gehen, Musik hören kann. CD-Player ist ein CD-Spieler. CD ist die Abkürzung für Compact Disc, also eine kompakte, kleine Schallplatte.

Seite 13–15

1.

Hello!	Hi, this is Lilly. Who's there?
It's me, Anne. How are you?	I'm fine, thanks, and you?
I'm fine too, thank you.	Tomorrow is my birthday.
Oh, right.	I'm having a party.
Super.	Are you coming?
Yes.	Great, see you tomorrow.
What time?	At five o'clock.
O.K. See you.	Bye.

2. Ben's number: 9191438, Tom's number: 38169, Mary's number: 73654

3. 856738 – eɪt faɪv sɪks 'sevn θriː eɪt, 255972 – tuː faɪv faɪv naɪn 'sevn tuː, 378165 – θriː 'sevn eɪt wʌn sɪks faɪv, 724314 – 'sevn tuː fɔː(r) θriː wʌn fɔː(r), 612381 – sɪks wʌn tuː θriː eɪt wʌn, 542348 – faɪv fɔː(r) tuː θriː fɔː(r) eɪt.

Seite 19–21

1. The baby is young.
The ladybird is small.
The girl is sad.
The boy is happy.
The bird is black.
The bear is big.
The witch is old.

2. new – old, white – black,
long – short, heavy – light,
small – big, happy – sad,
old – young, clean – dirty, left – right.

3. Lösungswort: GREAT!

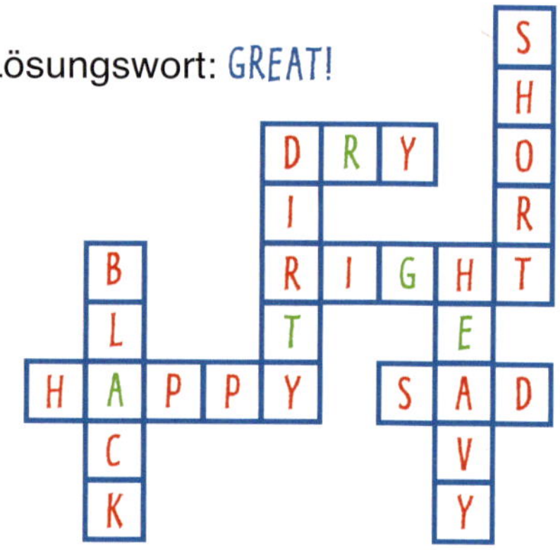

Seite 25–28

1. Bob is wearing a blue sweatshirt and green trousers. His shoes are brown.
Lilly is wearing a white T-shirt and a red skirt. Her shoes are blue.
Ben is wearing a yellow T-shirt and blue trousers. His shoes are black.
Anne is wearing a pink dress. Her shoes are green.

2. There are pink trousers. There's a green T-shirt. There's a yellow dress. There's a red coat. There's a brown sweatshirt. There are blue socks.

3. skirt, sweatshirt, T-shirt, trousers

5.

Seite 31–34

1.

2. The mouse said "no more" at four o'clock.
The mouse ran down at one o'clock.

3. It's a quarter past four.
It's a quarter past eight.
Excuse me, what's the time, please? It's half past nine.
Excuse me, what's the time, please? It's ten o'clock.

Doodoos Socken sind auf den Seiten 27 und 28.

4.

a quarter to ten

half past three

two o'clock

seven o'clock

a quarter past four

half past eleven

a quarter to two

six o'clock

Seite 37–40

1.  rubber  ruler  pencil  teacher  pupil

 classroom  desk

3.

p	e	b	a	x	y	z	u	p	e	n	l	a	d	i
d	f	b	n	r	o	g	s	l	p	v	q	c	o	n
e	d	o	v	r	u	l	e	r	e	g	j	m	c	d
k	y	o	x	t	k	k	d	b	a	o	b	c	h	o
l	a	k	r	i	v	y	k	u	p	t	e	f	a	q
s	u	z	s	c	h	o	o	l	b	a	g	v	l	u
m	d	e	z	u	s	m	p	r	l	d	h	i	k	p
a	d	f	h	j	o	s	y	l	a	n	t	e	b	y
p	e	p	u	r	h	q	u	i	c	n	o	c	a	f
u	b	y	d	e	s	k	s	a	k	r	n	h	b	e
p	j	o	h	s	b	e	r	y	b	l	n	a	x	i
i	x	c	r	y	s	a	g	z	o	k	v	i	c	b
l	a	z	t	s	u	w	u	l	a	m	t	r	h	o
o	t	e	a	c	h	e	r	i	r	d	e	l	i	o
t	a	e	g	c	u	l	m	o	d	r	a	g	l	l

Seite 43–46

1. There is a green egg on the table. There is a pink egg in the bowl. There is a grey egg next to the armchair. There is a red egg in front of the lamp. There is a blue egg under the rug. There is an orange egg between the books.

2. Doodoos Schwanz ist sechsmal zu sehen.

3. Lösungswort: in front of

Seite 49–52

1. I live in Great Britain. We are going on holiday to Germany.
I live in Italy. We are going on holiday to Austria.
I live in Germany. We are going on holiday to Italy.
I live in France. We are going on holiday to Belgium.

2.

3. Bob is going by bus.
Anne and Lilly are going by ship.
Judy is going by car.
Mary is going by plane.
Ben and Tom are going by train.

4. Lösungswort: HOLIDAY

			B			S	
			U			H	
			S	P	A	I	N
				L		P	
I		C		A			
T	R	A	I	N			
A		R		E			
L							
Y							

Seite 55–58

1. cat, broom, spider, Halloween, bat, witch

2. pumpkin, ghost, hat

3. Ben puts the butter, the sugar, a pinch of salt, the eggs, the flour, the baking powder, and the milk in a bowl.
Ben puts baking paper on a baking sheet.

4. Halloween is in October. It is in autumn.
Christmas is in December. It is in winter.

Seite 61–64

1. It's sunny in France. It's cloudy in Great Britain.
It's snowy in Austria. It's windy in Denmark.
It's rainy in the Netherlands. It's cloudy in Italy.
It's sunny in Spain. It's windy in Ireland.

2. It's windy.  It's rainy.  It's foggy. 

It's snowy.  It's sunny.  It's cloudy. 

3. It has two black eyes. It is holding a broom. Its nose is a carrot.
It has no legs. It has a black hat on the head. It is a SNOWMAN.

4. It was foggy on Thursday. It was rainy on Monday and on Friday.
It was sunny on Tuesday and on Monday. It was stormy on Saturday.
On Tuesday it was sunny. On Saturday it was stormy.
On Sunday it was windy. On Wednesday it was cloudy.

5. It's snowing. We need winter boots, an anorak, a hat and gloves.
RAINCOAT is the wrong word.
It's raining. We need an umbrella, rubber boots and a raincoat.
BATHING SUIT is the wrong word.
It's sunny. We need a bathing suit, sunglasses and a sunshade.
SCARF is the wrong word.
It's windy. We need a headband, a scarf, a jacket.
SUNGLASSES is the wrong word.

Seite 67–70

1. There is the frog.

2. He turns right. At the first crossing he turns left. At the second crossing he walks straight on. He crosses the street at the traffic lights. He walks straight on. At the first crossing he turns left and walks to the traffic lights. He crosses the street. There is the school.

3. Yes, you turn left and go straight on, at the first crossing you turn right.
Excuse me, can you tell me the way from the bus stop to the school, please? Yes, you go straight on. At the first crossing you turn left. There is the school.

4.

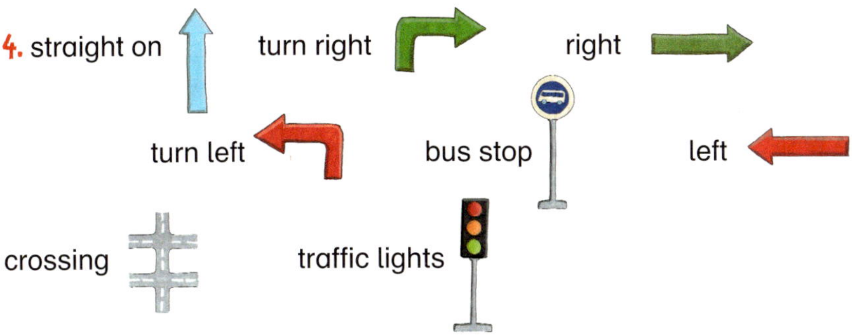

Wörterverzeichnis

Englisch – Deutsch

A, a

a	ein, eine
afternoon	Nachmittag
all	alle
alone	allein
along	entlang
alphabet	Alphabet
and	und
angel	Engel
animals	Tiere
anorak	Anorak
the answer to	die Antwort auf
apple	Apfel
April	April
Are you coming?	Kommst du?
arm	Arm
armchair	Sessel
at 10 o'clock	um 10 Uhr
at home	zu Hause
at school	in der Schule
attic	Dachboden
August	August
Austria	Österreich
autumn	Herbst

B, b

back	zurück
back	Rücken
baking paper	Backpapier
baking powder	Backpulver
baking sheet	Backblech
ball	Ball
banana	Banane
bat	Fledermaus
bath tub	Badewanne
bathing suit	Badeanzug
bathroom	Badezimmer
bear	Bär
bed	Bett
bedroom	Schlafzimmer
behind	hinter
Belgium	Belgien
belt	der Gürtel
better	besser
between	zwischen
big	groß
bird	Vogel
birthday	Geburtstag
black	schwarz
blackboard	Tafel
blue	blau
body	Körper
book	Buch
boot	Stiefel
bowl	Schüssel
boy	Junge
broom	Besen
brother	Bruder
brown	braun
bus	Bus
bus stop	Bushaltestelle
butter	Butter
to buzz	läuten
Bye!, Bye-bye!	Tschüss!, Auf Wiedersehen!

C, c

cake	Kuchen
calendar	Kalender
can	können
Can you find them?	Kannst du sie finden?
Can you tell me ...?	Kannst du mir sagen ...? Können Sie mir sagen ...?
cap	Kappe
car	Auto
cardboard	Pappe
carrot	Karotte
cat	Katze
to celebrate	feiern
certain	sicher
chair	Stuhl
chalk	Kreide
chapter	Kapitel
chimney	Kamin
Christmas	Weihnachten
to clap	klatschen
classroom	Klassenzimmer
clean	sauber
clock	Uhr
clothes	Kleider
cloud	Wolke
cloudy	bewölkt
coat	Mantel
cold	kalt
colour	Farbe
to colour	anmalen
to come	kommen
to complete	vervollständigen
complete	vollständig
to connect	verbinden
cow	Kuh
to cross	überqueren
crossing	Kreuzung
crossword puzzle	Kreuzworträtsel
cucumber	Gurke
curtain	Vorhang
to cut	schneiden
cutting board	Schneidebrett

D, d

day	Tag
dear	liebe, lieber
Dear me!	Oh je!
December	Dezember
to decorate	dekorieren
Denmark	Dänemark
desk	Schreibtisch, Pult
dirty	dreckig
doctor	Arzt
dog	Hund
Don't forget ...!	Vergiss nicht ...!
door	Tür
down	runter, unten
to draw	zeichnen
dress	Kleid
to drop	fallen lassen, aufgeben
dry	trocken

E, e

ear	Ohr
Easter	Ostern
to eat	essen
eight	acht
elbow	Ellbogen
elephant	Elefant
eleven	elf
entangled	verknotet, verwickelt
even now	selbst jetzt
evening	Abend
every	jeder, jede, jedes
excepting	außer
Excuse me …	Entschuldige …, Entschuldigen Sie …
exercise book	Schreibheft
eye	Auge

F, f

family	Familie
farm	Bauernhof
father	Vater
Father Christmas	Weihnachtsmann (in Großbritannien)
favourite	Lieblings…
to fear	fürchten
February	Februar
to fill in	ausfüllen
to find	finden
Find your way!	Finde deinen Weg!
finger	Finger
first	der, die, das Erste
fish	Fisch
five	fünf
floor	Stockwerk, Fußboden
flour	Mehl
flue	Grippe
fog	Nebel
foggy	neblig
to fold	falten
foot	Fuß
feet	Füße
for	für, zu
for dinner	zum Abendessen
to forget	vergessen
to form	formen
four	vier
France	Frankreich
free	frei
Friday	Freitag
friend	Freund, Freundin
frog	Frosch
from	aus, von
fruit	Obst
fruit salad	Obstsalat

G, g

game	Spiel
Germany	Deutschland
ghost	Geist
gingerbread	Lebkuchen
girl	Mädchen

to give	geben
gloves	Handschuhe
glue	kleben, Kleber
to go	gehen
to go shopping	einkaufen gehen
to go to bed	zu Bett gehen
to go to school	zur Schule gehen
good	gut
Goodbye!	Auf Wiedersehen!
Good morning!	Guten Morgen!
Good night!	Gute Nacht!
grandma	Oma, Großmutter
grapes	Trauben
great	toll
Great Britain	Großbritannien
green	grün
grey	grau
ground floor	Erdgeschoss
to guess	raten

H, h

half	halb
half past seven (!)	halb acht (!)
Halloween	Halloween
hand	Hand
happy	glücklich
Happy New Year!	Frohes neues Jahr!
to have to	müssen
hat	Hut, Mütze
to have	haben
he	er
he has …	er hat …
he has to …	er muss …
he is …	er ist …
head	Kopf
headband	Stirnband
heavy	schwer
Hello!	Hallo!
help	Hilfe
to help	helfen
Here you are!	Bitte sehr!
Hi!	Hey!, Hallo!
him	ihm, ihn
his	sein
to hold	halten
horse	Pferd
hot	heiß
house	Haus
How are you?	Wie geht es dir?
How many …?	Wie viele …?
howe'er/ however	wie auch immer
to hurry	sich beeilen
to hurt	wehtun

I, i

I	ich
I am …	Ich bin …
I am not …	Ich bin nicht …
I can see …	Ich kann (etwas) sehen.
I have …	Ich habe …
I mean …	Ich glaube …
I wish you …	Ich wünsche dir/ euch …

I'm fine.	Mir geht es gut.
I've got it!	Ich hab's!
icing	Zuckerguss
icing sugar	Puderzucker
if	wenn
ill	krank
impossible	unmöglich
in front of	vor
in German	auf Deutsch
in May	im Mai
to invite	einladen
Ireland	Irland
Is this …?	Ist das …?
It is …	Es ist …
It was …	Es war …
It's … o'clock.	Es ist … Uhr.
It's me.	Ich bin's.
Italy	Italien

J, j

January	Januar
jeans	Jeans
juice	Saft
July	July
jumper	Pulli
June	Juni

K, k

kitchen	Küche
knee	Knie
knife	Messer
to know	wissen

L, l

labyrinth	Labyrinth
ladybird	Marienkäfer
lamp	Lampe
late	spät
leap year	Schaltjahr
left	links
leg	Bein
lemon	Zitrone
Let's see …	Mal sehen …
letter	Brief, Buchstabe
light	leicht
line	Linie
lip	Lippe
little	klein
living room	Wohnzimmer
long	lang
Look at that!	Seht euch das an!
to look for	suchen
to lose	verlieren
lost	verloren
love	Liebe

M, m

to make	machen
March	März
May	Mai
medicine	Medizin
merry	fröhlich
mice	Mäuse
to mix	mischen
mixer	Handrührgerät
Monday	Montag

monkey	Affe
month	Monat
morning	Morgen
mother	Mutter
mouse	Maus
mouth	Mund
my	mein/meine
My name is …	Ich heiße …

N, n

name	Name
neck	Hals
need	brauchen
the Netherlands	die Niederlande
new	neu
next to	neben
night	Nacht
nine	neun
no	nein, keine
no more	genug
nose	Nase
November	November
now	jetzt
number	Zahl

O, o

O dear!	Oh je!
October	Oktober
of	von
of course	natürlich
off	aus, ab
old	alt
on	auf, am, an
on the farm	auf dem Bauernhof
on the telephone	am Telefon
Once there was …	Es war einmal …
one	eins, eine, einer
onion	Zwiebel
onto	auf
opposites	Gegensätze
or	oder
orange	Orange
orange	orange
(I) ought to …	(Ich) sollte …
own	eigener, eigene, eigenes

P, p

paper	Papier
paper hat	Papphut
pear	Birne
to peel	schälen
pen	Stift
pen friend	Brieffreund(in)
pencil	Bleistift
penguin	Pinguin
piano lesson	Klavierstunde
picture	Bild
piece	Stück
pig	Schwein
pinch of salt	Prise Salz
pineapple	Ananas
pink	rosa

plane	Flugzeug
to play	spielen
playtime	Spielzeit
please	bitte
poem	Gedicht
Portugal	Portugal
potato	Kartoffel
presents	Geschenke
pronunciation	Aussprache
pudding	Pudding
to pull	ziehen
pumpkin	Kürbis
pupil	Schüler, Schülerin
to put	setzen, stellen, legen
to put to bed	ins Bett legen

Q, q

quarter past	Viertel nach
quarter to	Viertel vor
question	Frage
quite	ganz, ziemlich

R, r

rabbit	Kaninchen
rain	Regen
raincoat	Regenmantel
rainy	regnerisch
to read	lesen
really	wirklich
red	rot
rest	Rest
right	rechts, richtig
Right!	Stimmt!
roof	Dach
room	Zimmer
rubber boots	Gummistiefel
rug	Teppich
ruler	Lineal
to run	rennen

S, s

sad	traurig
sandals	Sandalen
Santa Claus	Weihnachtsmann (in den USA)
Saturday	Samstag
to say	sagen
scarf	Schal
school	Schule
schoolbag	Schultasche
scissors	Schere
seasons	Jahreszeiten
second	der, die, das Zweite
to see	sehen
see you	bis dann
seeing the doctor	beim Arzt
September	September
seven	sieben
shelves	Regal
ship	Schiff
shoe	Schuh
shopping list	Einkaufsliste
short	kurz

shoulder	Schulter
to shout hurray	Hurra rufen
to show	zeigen
sister	Schwester
to sit	sitzen
six	sechs
skirt	Rock
sky	Himmel
small	klein
snake	Schlange
snow	Schnee
snowman	Schneemann
snowy	verschneit
socks	Socken
sofa	Sofa
some	etwas
song	Lied
Spain	Spanien
spider	Spinne
to spot	entdecken
spring	Frühling
to stamp	stampfen
star	Stern
stocking	Strumpf
stomach	Bauch
storm	Sturm
straight on	geradeaus
strawberry	Erdbeere
street	Straße
to strike	schlagen
summer	Sommer
summer holidays	Sommerferien
sun	Sonne
Sunday	Sonntag
sunglasses	Sonnenbrille
sunny	sonnig
sunshade	Sonnenschirm
sweatshirt	Sweatshirt
Switzerland	die Schweiz

T, t

T-shirt	T-Shirt
tablespoon	Esslöffel
tail	Schwanz
teacher	Lehrer, Lehrerin
teddybear	Teddybär
teeth	Zähne
telephone number	Telefonnummer
to tell	erzählen
ten	zehn
text	Text
thank you	danke
thanks	danke
the	der, die, das
them	ihnen
then	dann
There are …	Es gibt …
There are no …	Es gibt keine …
they	sie
They are …	Sie sind …
They are writing …	Sie schreiben …
They have …	Sie haben …
thin	dünn
thing	Ding
to think	denken
to think of	an etwas denken

this	dies
This is …	Dies ist …
three	drei
through	durch
Thursday	Donnerstag
tiger	Tiger
time	Zeit
timetable	Stundenplan
to	zu
toe	Zeh
toilet	Toilette
tomato	Tomate
tomorrow	morgen
tongue	Zunge
too	auch
traffic lights	Ampel
train	Zug
tree	Baum
trousers	Hose
trunk	Rüssel
to try	versuchen
Tuesday	Dienstag
turkey	Truthahn
to turn	abbiegen
twelve	zwölf
two	zwei

U, u

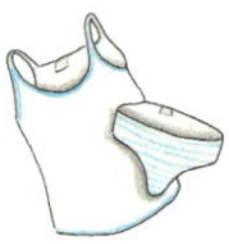

umbrella	Regenschirm
under	unter
underwear	Unterwäsche
up	hinauf
to use	verwenden

V, v

vegetables	Gemüse
vocabulary	Wörterliste

W, w

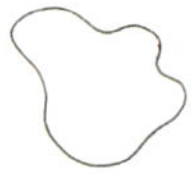

want	wollen
wardrobe	Schrank
washing line	Wäscheleine
washing machine	Waschmaschine
watch	Armbanduhr
water	Wasser
way	Weg
we	wir
We can't …	Wir können nicht …
to wear	tragen (Kleidung)
weather	Wetter
weather chart	Wetterliste
weather forecast	Wettervorhersage
Wednesday	Mittwoch
week	Woche
weekend	Wochenende
(he) went	(er) ging
wet	nass
what	was
when	wenn
Where are …?	Wo sind …?
where to go	wohin
which	die, welche
white	weiß
who	wer

Who is this?	Wer ist das?
Who's there?	Wer ist dort?
wind	Wind
window	Fenster
windy	windig
winner	Gewinner
winter	Winter
winter boots	Winterstiefel
witch	Hexe
with	mit
word	Wort
to write	schreiben
Write soon!	Schreib bald!
wrong	falsch

Y, y

yellow	gelb
yes	ja
you	du
You are …	Du bist …
You can …	Du kannst …
young	jung
your	dein, deine
Yummie!	Mmmh, lecker!

Z, z

zebra	Zebra

Deutsch – Englisch

A, a

ab	off
abbiegen	to turn
Abend	evening
acht	eight
Affe	monkey
alle	all
Alphabet	alphabet
alt	old
am Telefon	on the telephone
Ampel	traffic lights
Ananas	pineapple
anmalen	to colour
Anorak	anorak
Antwort auf	answer to
Apfel	apple
April	April
Arm	arm
Armbanduhr	watch
Arzt	doctor
auch	too
auf	onto
Auf Wiedersehen!	Goodbye!
auf, am, an	on
aufgeben	to drop
Auge	eye
August	August
aus	off, from
ausfüllen	to fill in
außer	excepting
Auto	car

B, b

Backblech	baking sheet
Backpapier	baking paper
Backpulver	baking powder
Badeanzug	bathing suit
Badewanne	bath tub
Badezimmer	bathroom
Ball	ball
Banane	banana
Bär	bear
Bauch	stomach
Bauernhof	farm
Baum	tree
beim Arzt	seeing the doctor
Bein	leg
Belgien	Belgium
Besen	broom
besser	better
Bett	bed
bewölkt	cloudy
Bild	picture
Birne	pear
Bis dann!	See you!
bitte	please
Bitte sehr!	Here you are!
blau	blue
Bleistift	pencil
brauchen	need
braun	brown
Brief	letter
Brieffreund, Brieffreundin	pen friend
Bruder	brother
Buch	book
Buchstabe	letter
Bus	bus
Bushaltestelle	bus stop
Butter	butter

D, d

Dach	roof
Dachboden	attic
Dänemark	Denmark
danke	thank you
danke	thanks
dann	then
das	the
dein, deine	your
dekorieren	to decorate
denken	to think
(an etwas) denken	to think of
der	the
Deutschland	Germany
Dezember	December
die	the
die, welche	which
Dienstag	Tuesday
dies	this
Dies ist …	This is …
Telefonnummer	telephone number
Ding	thing
Donnerstag	Thursday
dreckig	dirty
drei	three
du	you

dünn	thin
durch	through

E, e

eigener, eigene, eigenes	own
ein, eine	a
einkaufen gehen	to go shopping
Einkaufsliste	shopping list
eins, eine, einer	one
Elefant	elephant
elf	eleven
Ellbogen	elbow
Engel	angel
entdecken	to spot
entlang	along
Entschuldige/ entschuldigen Sie …	Excuse me …
er	he
Er hat …	He has …
Er ist …	He is …
Er muss …	He has to …
Erdbeere	strawberry
Erdgeschoss	ground floor
Erste, der, die, das	first, the
erzählen	to tell
Es gibt keine …	There are no …
Es gibt …	There are …
Es war einmal …	Once there was ...
essen	to eat
Esslöffel	tablespoon
etwas	some
etwas benutzen	to use something

F, f

fallen lassen	to drop
falsch	wrong
falten	to fold
Familie	family
Farbe	colour
Februar	February
feiern	to celebrate
Fenster	window
finden	to find
Finger	finger
Fisch	fish
Fledermaus	bat
Flugzeug	plane
formen	to form
Frage	question
Frankreich	France
frei	free
Freitag	Friday
Freund, Freundin	friend
Frohes neues Jahr!	Happy New Year!
fröhlich	merry
Frosch	frog
Frühling	spring
fünf	five
für, zu	for
fürchten	to fear
Fuß	foot

die Füße	feet
der Fußboden	floor

G, g

ganz	quite
geben	to give
Geburtstag	birthday
Gedicht	poem
Gegensätze	opposites
gehen	to go
Geist	ghost
gelb	yellow
Gemüse	vegetable(s)
genug	no more
geradeaus	straight on
Geschenke	presents
Gewinner	winner
ging	(he) went
glücklich	happy
grau	grey
Grippe	flue
groß	big
Großbritannien	Great Britain
Großmutter	grandma
grün	green
Gummistiefel	rubber boots
Gurke	cucumber
Gürtel	belt
gut	good
Gute Nacht!	Good night!
Guten Morgen!	Good morning!

H, h

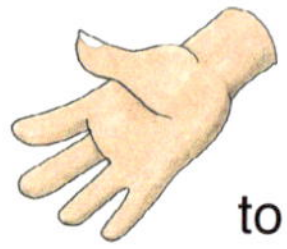

haben	to have
halb	half
halb acht (!)	half past seven (!)
halten	to hold
Hallo!	Hello!
Halloween	Halloween
Hals	neck
Hand	hand
Handrührgerät	mixer
Handschuhe	gloves
Haus	house
heiß	hot
helfen	to help
Herbst	autumn
Hexe	witch
Hey!, Hallo!	Hi!
Hilfe	help
Himmel	sky
hinauf	up
hinter	behind
Hose	trousers
Hund	dog
Hurra!	Hurray!
Hut	hat

I, i

Ich heiße …	My name is …
ihm, ihn	him
ihnen	them
in der Schule	at school
ins Bett legen, zu Bett bringen	to put to bed

J, j

ja	yes
Jahr	year
Jahreszeiten	seasons
jeder, jede, jedes	every
jetzt	now
jung	young
Junge	boy

K, k

Kalender	calendar
kalt	cold
Kamin	chimney
Kaninchen	rabbit
Kapitel	chapter
Kappe	cap
Karotte	carrot
Kartoffel	potato
Katze	cat
Klassenzimmer	classroom
klatschen	to clap
Klavierstunde	piano lesson
kleben, Kleber	(to) glue
Kleid	dress
Kleider	clothes
klein	little, small
Knallbonbon	Christmas cracker
kommen	to come
Kommst du?	Are you coming?
können	can
Können Sie mir sagen …	Can you tell me …
Kopf	head
Körper	body
Kreide	chalk
Kreuzung	crossing
Kreuzworträtsel	crossword puzzle
Kuchen	cake
Kuh	cow
Kürbis	pumpkin
kurz	short

L, l

Labyrinth	labyrinth
Lampe	lamp
lang	long
läuten	to buzz
Lebkuchen	gingerbread
Lehrer, Lehrerin	teacher
leicht	light
lesen	to read
Liebe	love
liebe, lieber	dear
Lieblings…	favourite
Lied	song
Lineal	ruler
Linie	line
links	left
Lippe	lip

M, m

machen	to make
Mädchen	girl

Mai	May
Mal sehen …	Let's see …
Mantel	coat
Marienkäfer	ladybird
März	March
Maus	mouse
Mäuse	mice
Medizin	medicine
Mehl	flour
mein, meine	my
mischen	to mix
mit	with
Mittwoch	Wednesday
Monat	month
Montag	Monday
Morgen	morning
morgen	tomorrow
Mund	mouth
müssen	to have to
Mutter	mother
Mütze	hat

N, n

Nachmittag	afternoon
Nacht	night
Name	name
Nase	nose
nass	wet
natürlich	of course
Nebel	fog
neben	next to
neblig	foggy
nein	no
neu	new
neun	nine
Niederlande, die	Netherlands, the
November	November

O, o

Obst	fruit
Obstsalat	fruit salad
oder	or
Ohr	ear
Oktober	October
Oma	grandma
Orange	orange
orange	orange
Ostern	Easter
Österreich	Austria
Ostersonntag	Easter Sunday

P, p

Papier	paper
Pappe	cardboard
Papphut	paper hat
Pferd	horse
Pinguin	penguin
Portugal	Portugal
Prise Salz	pinch of salt
Pudding	pudding
Pult	desk

R, r

raten	to guess
rechts	right
Regal	shelves
Regen	rain
Regenmantel	raincoat
Regenschirm	umbrella
regnerisch	rainy
rennen	to run
Rest	rest
richtig	right
Rock	skirt
rosa	pink
rot	red
Rücken	back
rufen	to shout
runter, unten	down
Rüssel	trunk

S, s

sagen	say
Samstag	Saturday
Sandalen	sandals
sauber	clean
Schal	scarf
schälen	peel
Schaltjahr	leap year
Schere	scissors
Schiff	ship
Schlafzimmer	bedroom
schlagen	to strike
Schlange	snake
Schneemann	snowman
Schneidebrett	cutting board
schneiden	to cut
Schnee	snow
Schrank	wardrobe
Schreib bald!	Write soon!
schreiben	write
Schreibheft	exercise book
Schreibtisch	desk
Schuh	shoe
Schule	school
Schüler, Schülerin	pupil
Schultasche	schoolbag
Schulter	shoulder
Schüssel	bowl
Schwanz	tail
schwarz	black
Schwein	pig
Schweiz, die	Switzerland
schwer	heavy
Schwester	sister
sechs	six
sehen	to see
sein	his
selbst jetzt	even now
September	September
Sessel	armchair
setzen, stellen, legen	to put
sich beeilen	to hurry
sicher	certain
sie	they
Sie haben …	They have …
Sie schreiben …	They are writing …

Sie sind …	They are …
sieben	seven
sitzen	to sit
Socken	socks
Sofa	sofa
Sohn	son
sollte	(I) ought to
Sommer	summer
Sommerferien	summer holidays
Sonne	sun
Sonnenbrille	sunglasses
Sonnenschirm	sunshade
sonnig	sunny
Sonntag	Sunday
Spanien	Spain
spät	late
Spiel	game
spielen	to play
Spielzeit	playtime
Spinne	spider
stampfen	to stamp
Stern	star
Stiefel	boot
Stift	pen
stimmt	right
Stirnband	headband
Stockwerk	floor
Straße	street
Strumpf	stocking
Stück	piece
Stuhl	chair
Stundenplan	timetable
Sturm	storm
stürmisch	stormy
suchen	to look for
Sweatshirt	sweatshirt

T, t

T-Shirt	T-shirt
Tafel	blackboard
Tag	day
Teddybär	teddybear
Teppich	rug
Text	text
Tier	animal
Tiger	tiger
Toilette	toilet
toll	great
Tomate	tomato
tragen (Kleidung)	to wear
Trauben	grapes
traurig	sad
trocken	dry
Truthahn	turkey
Tschüss!, Auf Wiedersehen!	Bye, Bye-bye!
Tür	door

U, u

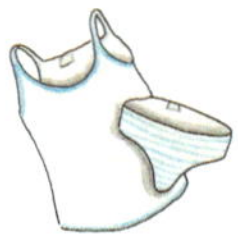

überqueren	to cross
Uhr	clock
und	and
unter	under
Unterwäsche	underwear

V, v

Vater	father
verbinden	to connect
vergessen	to forget
vergiss nicht	don't forget
verknotet	entangled
verlieren	to lose
verloren	lost
verschneit	snowy
versuchen	to try
vervollständigen	to complete
verwenden	to use
verwickelt	entangled
vier	four
Viertel nach	quarter past
Viertel vor	quarter to
Vogel	bird
vollständig	complete
von	of
von	from
Vorhang	curtain

W, w

was	what
Wäscheleine	washing line
Waschmaschine	washing machine
Wasser	water
Weg	way
Weihnachten	Christmas
Weihnachtsmann	Santa Claus, Father Christmas
weiß	white
wenn	when
wer	who
Wer ist das?	Who is this?
Wer ist dort?	Who's there?
Wetter	weather
weather chart	Wetterliste
Wettervorhersage	weather forecast
Wie geht es dir?	How are you?
Wie heißt du?	What's your name?
Wie ist ...?	What's ... like?
Wie ist/lautet deine Nummer?	What's your number?
Wie viele ...?	How many ...?
Wie viel Uhr ist es?	What time is it?
Um wie viel Uhr?	What time?
Wind	wind
windig	windy
Winter	winter
Winterstiefel	winter boots
wir	we
Wir können ... nicht ...	We can't ...
wirklich	really
Wo sind ...?	Where are ...?
Woche	week
Wochenende	weekend
wohin	where to go
Wohnzimmer	living room
Wolke	cloud
wollen	want
Wort	word
Wörterliste	vocabulary

Z, z

Zahl	number
Zähne	teeth
Zebra	zebra
Zeh	toe
zehn	ten
zeichnen	to draw
zeigen	to show
Zeit	time
ziehen	to pull
ziemlich	quite
Zimmer	room
Zitrone	lemon
zu	to
zu Bett gehen	to go to bed
zu Hause	at home
Zug	train
zum Abendessen	for dinner
Zunge	tongue
zur Schule gehen	to go to school
zurück	back
zwei	two
Zweite, der, die, das	the second
Zwiebel	onion
zwischen	between
zwölf	twelve